Enjoy the Journey through...!

Forty Days of Grace

A Prayer Devotional

by Kim Y. Jackson

Elder Kim Jackson

"Forty Days of Grace"

Publishing and Cover Design by
God's Glory Publishing

Interior Layout Design by Joy E. Turner
JetSet Communications & Consulting

ISBN # 0-974374938
ISBN 13# 978-0-9743749-3-2

Dedication

This book is dedicated to the *men* and *women* of God who believe that in the latter days there still remains a need for prayer and fasting within the Kingdom of God. Sacrificing and sanctification to hear clearer the instructions from the Lord is not to be taken lightly. Today unlike never before the church of the Living God needs to "Hear What the Spirit says to the Church." I praise God for His chosen elect who have purposed in their hearts to make a commitment to *prayer* and *fasting* for Forty Days. These are those who shall witness the manifestation of His Glory and walk in His Grace. Hallelujah to the King of Kings and the Lord of Lord.

Acknowledgments

Heavenly Father I thank you for entrusting me with the gift of a scribe to write, receive revelation knowledge and to discern that there is a time and a season for everything. This book is written at the end of and beginning to a new season of God's purpose being fulfilled in my life. Lord I can't imagine my life without you. Thank you for giving me this gift, which I pray will always give you the Glory.

I praise God for women who impart God's word, implement His plan and are part of God's divine plan to fulfill His promises. Their obedience has changed a nation. The purpose and power of God lies within you for a time such as this. May the Blessings of the Lord Overtake You!!!

I thank God for each and every one of the women who sacrificed, consecrated and witnessed God's miracles manifested, individually as well as corporately. God's word declares in Isaiah 1:19 "if you are willing and obedient you shall eat the good of the land." Through these forty days of prayer and fasting we have seen God elevate us into places of destiny never seen before. We have witnessed curses destroyed, burdens lifted, restoration, territory claimed and liberty to the captive. This could only have been done through the Grace of God. Hallelujah, Hallelujah, Hallelujah!!! Praise be unto our God.

I thank God for my son Ryan's love, support, compassion, and creativity. It's been a pleasure to work with you on this project and watch you mature in your gifts. To God be the Glory.

I acknowledge my grandson Russell who helped to develop the cover for the re-release of 40 Days of Grace. He has been touched with the gift of vision.

Foreword

This book was written to celebrate the manifestation of God's word. Bishop J. Charles Carrington, Jr. had instructed the congregation, to declare God's word concerning every area of our lives. The Lord declared in His word that we can "speak those things that are not as though they were." God had also reminded us to "write the vision and make it plain." Throughout this journey He released in our hearts that "eyes have not seen, nor ears heard, neither entered into the hearts of man, the things He has prepared for them that love Him", 1 Corinthians 2:9. I thank the Lord for this journey and every word He has spoken. We have found in His Word that He has moved us from a position where "His grace is sufficient" to us living in His "Abundant Grace." Walking in this new day, with God we submit to God and release Him to speak words of life, edification and purpose as we pray, fast and praise Him for "His Grace." The word God has spoken during this journey is a declaration from God to His people of His many promises and might. Bless the name of Jesus!

Table of Contents

Dedication..iii

Acknowledgments...iv

Foreword...v

Introduction...8

Fasting God's Way..9

The Call for Grace...15

Forty Day - Prayer/Devotional.......…................................ 17

    Day 1 - His Grace is Sufficient......................................18
    Day 2 - Renewing of your mind......................................21
    Day 3 - My Healer..24
    Day 4 - Faith without Works is Dead..............................27
    Day 5 - The Miracle Worker..30
    Day 6 - God's Love...33
    Day 7 - Exceeding and Great Joy....................................36
    Day 8 - Rest..39
    Day 9 - If He said it, will He not do it............................42
    Day 10 - The exchange...45
    Day 11 - Preparation for Fulfillment...............................48
    Day 12 - God's word concerning you...............................51
    Day 13 - Get the vision...54
    Day 14 - Strength for the Weary......................................57
    Day 15 - A Pastor's Heart..60
    Day 16 - God's order...63
    Day 17 - I can do all things...66
    Day 18 - Draw unto God..69
    Day 19 - His strength is made perfect..............................72
    Day 20 - Peace in the Storm..75

Day 21 - God's Faithfulness..78
Day 22 - Restoration...81
Day 23 - Set the Precedent...84
Day 24 - No more Struggles..87
Day 25 - Victory..90
Day 26 - Laying at His feet...93
Day 27 - Guard your heart..96
Day 28 - Behold the works of His hands................................99
Day 29 - Thy will be done...102
Day 30 - Looking for Love, He loved us First......................105
Day 31 - A Season to bear Fruit...108
Day 32 - Decently and in Order..111
Day 33 - Do the work of the Lord.......................................114
Day 34 - The Chastening of the Lord..................................117
Day 35 - The Transcendental Life.......................................120
Day 36 - Strengthen thy Brethren..123
Day 37 - God's Favor...126
Day 38 - He will dispatch His Angels..................................129
Day 39 - Unexpected Blessings...132
Day 40 - Abundant Grace..135

Conclusion 138

About the Author...139

Introduction

The "Forty Days of Grace" prayer devotional was inspired by God during a Forty Day Fast. Within the contents of this book you will find each step God carefully orchestrated to manifest love, healing, power and deliverance. God revealed these words to His servant, to share with His people. These words are written in remembrance of the hope found in Jesus Christ. Through prayer and fasting, God's people will be able to partake in the promises of God for a chosen nation. Each day God's words is made known, so that the nation that called upon the name of the Lord, would have a tabernacle of God's revelation and promises for this season of their lives. "Thanks be to God who gives us the victory through our Lord Jesus Christ", 1 Corinthians 15:57.

Fasting - God's Way

To record the word of the Lord while fasting is an honor and a privilege. Even more significant are the Biblical teachings found on Fasting. Each teaching gives the reader a greater understanding of Fasting - *God's Way*. As He has given us the ability to fast, we as believers in Christ must know what is entailed in fasting. The answers to some questions on prayer and fasting are revealed below.

Origin
During biblical times the Jews fasted yearly unto the Lord to commemorate a particular event in history, such as the Day of Atonement. They consecrated themselves and stood in agreement for the power of God to deliver them. The word fasting is mentioned over 70 times in the word of God, and specifically it is mentioned throughout the book of Acts.

Definition
The Hebrew word for fasting is "nesteia" and it means, "to not eat." Fasting is not always associated with not eating. However it is a form of self-denial.

Types of fasts:
Christians often fast from food. But they are not limited to abstaining from food. Many believers fast from food, television, sexual relations with husbands and wives upon agreement, negative habits, destructive habits and other things with great influence upon the lives of the believer.

Purpose of Fasting
Fasting is a voluntary biblical principal that is not to be confused with a diet. It is the believer's act of surrendering our focus and attention unto God. Often believer fasts to cleanse the mind and or physical body. Some fast to be more attuned to the voice of God and to intensify sensitivity in the Spirit. Many others fast to cultivate a deeper relationship with God.

Why Fast

Each believer has his or her own reason for fasting. For whatever the reason you have for fasting, you will find that it always revolves around knowing the mind of God. He already knows why we fast. He is looking for our willful act of obedience to seek Him and not man. The scriptures tell us that, "There are some things that can only be revealed by prayer and fasting", as indicated in Mark 9:29. Believe it. We cannot fast without prayer. Prayer and fasting work hand in hand. Prayer is the most integral part of our relationship with our Lord and Savior Jesus Christ. When we fast without praying our communication with God to receive the prayers of the righteous is disconnected, because there is no communication from us to Him.

When we commit our lives to prayer we open the lines of communication from the heart of a servant to our Lord. Dwelling here in His secret place of communion, God unveils His answers to your prayers and fasting. When the believer fasts God gives us not just temporary grace. He releases a permanent lifestyle change.

Prayer and fasting must also be accompanied by repentance. It is the act of acknowledging, confessing and turning from our sin, as well as asking for forgiveness. Unconfessed sin disconnects the believer from God. Repentance bridges the gap and enables reconciliation to God. Like fasting, prayer and repentance all play a major part in the life of every believer in Christ. Through fasting God exposes your sinful nature that displease Him. The remedy to being delivered from our sinful nature is called self-denial, obtainable only through prayer.

Self Denial

Those who fast humble themselves before God and yield their personal desires in exchange for self-denial. For the believer, self-denial is the act by which we submit ourselves to God. He in turn takes our selfish motives and carnal thoughts and subjects them for purification. God's refiner's fire burns away our carnal thoughts, lustful cravings, our judgments of others, self-indulgence and helps us to deal with the temptations we encounter.

Going through the purifying work of the refiner's fire, the children of God come forth as pure gold, according to Job 23:10. While in the fire God is ever mindful to watch the strength of the heat, length of the time within the heat and the type of heat we are processed in. At the right time God's fire is doused and the process is halted temporarily, for another time to come. We then become purified vessels ready for use by the watchman of the fire. We become ready for Him to "answer us and tell us the great and unsearchable things we do not know,' according to Jeremiah 33:3. The strength, length and type of fire have all been gauged to transform imperfections within each of us.

As we go though God's purification process through self-denial, we are lead by the Holy Spirit. By following the Holy Spirit we fulfill God's will.

Biblical examples of Fasting and its Benefits
The act of fasting is found many times throughout the bible. Each documented fast reveals God's sovereign will and sovereign power. Daniel's obedience as recorded in the Daniel 10:2 fast resulted in him becoming an interpreter of dreams. According to 1 Kings Chapter 19, Elijah fasted and by faith received strength and instructions for a nation. Moses fasted on a mountaintop according to Exodus 24:18. The direction he received required God's people to give an offering unto the Lord and to make way for God to dwell among His people. The second notation of Moses' fasting enabled him to receive the Ten Commandments that would be upheld throughout eternity. In Luke 2:37, Anna fasted and prayed resulting in her prophesying the birth of Jesus Christ - the Messiah. She also witnessed the presentation of Jesus at the temple. Acts 37:5 notes the story of Paul and other shipmates finding land after fasting through a violent storm. Another story in the Bible reveals how the Holy Spirit declared the setting apart of Saul and Barnabas for the work to which God had called them to perform, This occurred after they had fasted and prayed as recorded in Acts.

11

How to Fast
God gives the believer in Christ instructions on how to fast in the scriptures. According to Matthew 6:16-18, "When you fast, do not look somber as the hypocrites do, for they disfigure their faces to show men they are fasting. I tell you the truth, they have received their reward in full. But when you fast, put oil on your head and wash your face, so that it will not be obvious to men that you are fasting, but only to your Father, who is unseen; and your Father, who sees what is done in secret, will reward you openly." Fasting requires extreme discipline. It is a personal as well as private choice. Jesus gives us instructions not to show any outward appearance of fasting. By anointing our head we are asking God to give us His supernatural power to sustain us daily and to reveal his supernatural revelation for our lives.

The Daniel Fast
The Daniel fast was conducted according to Daniel 1:8. It consisted of fasting with no consumption of meat. To be compliant in this fast the believer had a diet consisting of only fruit, vegetables and water.

The Significance of 40 Days
The number forty has biblical significance. As illustrated in the bible the number forty was used during trials, testing and periods of judgment.

Major things happened as a result of praying and fasting for 40 days. According to Jonah 3:4, Ninevah was over thrown after forty days. Esther 4:16 tells of freedom for a nation after forty days. Blind Saul from the Damascus Road fasted for forty days according to Acts 9:9, and was healed. At the end of forty days of rain, Noah opened the widow in the Ark, according to Genesis 8:6. The scriptures tell us that in Acts 1:3 Jesus revealed himself for over forty days to speak about the Kingdom of God.

Revelation to the Nations
Through prayer and fasting for Forty Days, supernatural life changing power was received. There were a multitude of praise

reports and testimonials. Many people told of God saving family members, financial breakthroughs, deliverance from oppression and depression, families being reconciled, healings of the mind-body- and spirit, fulfillment of God's promises, birthing of spiritual gifts, ministries revealed, receipt of God's direction and wisdom, doors opening, overcoming fears, strong holds pulled down, and Victory over the adversary. We serve a mighty God. He wanted His nations to witness and partake of His Abundant Grace as we walked in obedience. When we seek after the face of God and no other, He promises that "He is a rewarder of them that diligently seek Him," found in Hebrews 11:6.

God's Demonstration of Abundant Grace

In the Forty Days of Grace - Day Prayer/Devotional located in the next section, God discloses His revelation and the journey orchestrated for nations of fasting believers. He manifests the demonstration of His power through deliverance. Divine revelation is witnessed by all that partake in individual and corporate fasts.

Scriptural Prayers for Fasting

As stated previously, prayer is of the utmost significance during fasting. You can't fast without praying. Scriptures found directly in the bible that can be used during fasting include Isaiah 58:6, which declares, "is not this kind of fasting I have chose: to loose the chains of injustice and untie the cords of the yoke, to set the oppressed free and break every yoke."

In addition Romans 8:26-27 states, "In the same way, the Spirit helps us in our weakness." We do not know what we ought to pray for, but the Spirit himself intercedes for us with groans that words cannot express." There are plenty of other scriptures from the bible that can be used as prayers. It is advised that you choose and use God's word when you pray. His word "does not return unto Him void and will accomplish what He pleases," Isaiah 55:11. When we use the word of God in prayer, we are backed up the authority of Jesus' Name.

The Call for Grace!

There is not a time in our lives where we do not need the Grace of God. Grace is God's enablement for His people to function and live. Yes, Grace is the unmerited favor of God, unlike God's mercy that keeps us from receiving what we are really due. The bible declares in Hebrews 4:1, Let us therefore come boldly to the throne of grace that we may obtain mercy and find grace to help in the time of need. So therefore we know that the gift of God's grace is available to all those that embrace and believe in the Lord Jesus Christ. How often have we attempted to complete a task only to recognize that the task could only be accomplished through the grace of God? Grace enables the exceeding abundantly above all that we could ask or think. Grace opens the doors that no man can open. It is God's grace that empowers us to live the life He's promised to us and that life more abundantly. When we recognize the significance of the grace of God, we come to the knowledge where our lives are no longer our own, that God is our ever present help in the time of trouble, and that it is in Him that we live move and have our being. Grace covers, grace sustains. Grace keeps us when the world is in turmoil.

As the scripture states we can "come boldly to the throne of Grace." It is before the throne of Grace where we are welcomed to enter into the presence of God and come to have an intimate encounter with the King of Kings, The Lord of Lords, our Savior. This place of God's Grace is where we lay down our troubles, concerns and fears, to receive the reassurance of Jesus Christ's love, compassion and sovereign ability. Grace is accessed through prayer which is the key to the answers we seek and the fulfillment of the desires of our heart. As God's people pray, God's ear is attuned to the petitions of His people, the sovereign will of God is manifested and lives are changed.

Forty is a number that represents testing and in some cases judgment. The bible tells us that for Forty Days Jesus was lead by the Spirit of the Lord, Noah experienced the rains while on the Ark, Moses was with God in the mountains, the spies searched the land, God gave Nineveh this time to repent and Jesus fasted for forty days and nights. These stories of forty days of obedience will last throughout eternity. For forty days there was a unified call for God's Grace to be upon a nation to be equipped, empowered and redeemed. The evidence of the manifestation of God's grace is revealed within the pages of Forty Days of Grace.

Forty Days of Grace

A Prayer Devotional

Day 1
His Grace is Sufficient
(2 Corinthians 12:9)

In the midst of your daily walk you often see circumstances you desire God to either remove you from or exercise His power and authority to deliver you out of. Be confident in our Sovereign Lord. He knows what is best for you. He will do for you what no one else can or will do for you. As you grow in Him you will come to know that "His Grace is Sufficient unto thee."

Day 1 - Prayer

Dear Lord, thank you for your sovereignty , and for being the author and finisher of my faith. There have been some circumstances that have not turned out the way I have wanted them to be, but I know that "you have the plans for me - to prosper and not to harm, for a future and a hope." With a grateful heart I know that He who watches over Israel neither slumbers nor sleeps. Right now you are restoring my soul and releasing an attitude of gratitude. Father you said in your word, "Have you considered my servant Job." And surely you have also considered me as one who walks in your grace and endures for the sake of the cross. Thank you for calling me to be your servant and to partake in your suffering as well as your resurrection. Thank you for declaring that my present sufferings are not worthy to be compared to the Glory that will be revealed in me. No one can ever do what you do, when you do, how you do, like you do for me. Throughout each encounter I have come to know that "Your Grace is Sufficient." In Jesus' Holy Name. Amen.

My Prayer Requests for Today

Day 2
Renewing of your mind
(Romans 12:2)

Children of God are often challenged by their old nature and old way of thinking. The mind is affected when we don't relinquish our old way and nature into the hands of All Mighty God. It is good to know that God has all authority over everything including your mind. Ask Him to take dominion over your mind. Seek after Him for the "renewing of your mind."

Day 2 - Prayer

Dear Gracious God, I magnify your Holy name. Today I thank you for a new beginning. This is the day that you have made and I will rejoice and be glad in it. Lord you continue to be my strength. You have set my feet upon a rock. You have shown me that you are able to do exceedingly and abundantly above all that I can ask or think, and it is according to the power that works within me. You have created in me a clean heart and renewed a right Spirit within me. You are transforming me into your image after your likeness. Thank you for reorganizing me and everything that surrounds me. I have waited patiently for you to make this change take place within me. Today you've shown me your power and ability to change my walk, talk and how I think. You, Oh Lord are emptying me so that you can put your new wine into this new wineskin. Thank you for the renewing of my mind.

My Prayer Requests for Today

_____

_____

_____

_____

_____

_____

_____

_____

_____

Day 3
My Healer
(Exodus 15:26)

By Faith believers in Christ, call upon Jehovah-Rophe - our Healer. We do this because of our desire to have a supernatural intervention of God's abilities within our physical bodies. The immediate deliverance of our infirmity is of the utmost importance. Deliverance from sickness, illness or disease is consistently on our minds and it is the focus of our prayers. Know that there is a natural desire for God to heal you, right now. Jesus our healer took thirty-nine stripes for your healing. Be mindful to seek after the Healer with as much fervor as you seek after the healing.

Day 3 - Prayer

Dear Lord, I Love You. I come before your throne of Grace to give you the Glory and Honor. You are perfect in all of your ways. It is in you that I put my trust. You promised in your word that no good thing would you withhold from them that walk uprightly before you. I come to you my healer, petitioning for my spiritual, physical and mental healing. You said that Jesus was wounded for our transgressions and He was bruised for our iniquities and the chastisement of our peace was upon Him and by His stripes I am healed. I know that you have all power in your hands. So I submit every aspect of my infirmities unto you, knowing that they must come into alignment with the Spirit of Christ that dwells within me. Where the Spirit of the Lord is there is Liberty. I come rejoicing in your might and I know that you are "the God that Healeth Thee." I give the all the Praise. In Jesus' Holy Name.

My Prayer Requests for Today

_____

_____

_____

_____

_____

_____

_____

_____

_____

Day 4
Faith without Works is Dead
(James 2:26)

Today remember to faithfully serve the Most High God. Faithfully commit to do the work that God has placed within your hands. By faith acknowledge that Jesus is the inspiration, by which we pursue and complete the works of our calling. By faith Jesus died for our sin. Don't let Jesus' death be in vain, because "Faith without Works is Dead."

Day 4 - Prayer

Dear Lord, Blessed be your Holy name. You are highly exalted above heaven and earth. I will praise your name forever. You have been faithful unto me. And it is my earnest desire to be faithful over every assignment that you have given to me. I recognize that it is a privilege for you to call me to perform a work in your name. Lord I want to complete your work faithfully. Daily I recognize God that I am walking by faith and not by sight to fulfill your designed plan. By faith, Noah built an ark, Abraham offered Isaac as a sacrifice, your people passed through the Red Sea, the walls of Jericho came down, Rahab the prostitute welcomed the spies, and your prophets gained what was promised. I desire this faith and I believe that faith is the substance of things hoped for and the evidence of things not seen. Lord help me to always conduct your work in faith, and let there be no work you have called me to do go undone. I shall do the work you have called me to do by Faith. In Jesus' Name.

My Prayer Requests for Today

_____

_____

_____

_____

_____

_____

_____

_____

_____

_____

Day 5
The Miracle Worker
(Acts 19:11)

In the life of every Christian there will be situations where you will desire God to perform a miracle. He performs miracles based upon His word written in the Gospels of Matthew, Mark, Luke and John. God specializes in miracles. He is more than able and absolutely capable of performing miracles. Trust in God to perform a miracle for you and through you today. You are His living miracle.

Day 5 – Prayer

Heavenly Father, you are the same God yesterday, today and forever more. And for that I give you the Glory. This day I seek after your grace and mercy to perform a miracle. I know that you have declared that the things that seem impossible with man are possible with you. Thank you Lord, for I trust and believe in your word. Because of your word Oh Lord, I don't have to wonder whether this miracle can be done. I know that it is done and that you have done it. Just like you performed extraordinary miracles through Paul you will also perform them through and for me. Lord, I believe that Jesus has done all of these miracles and I believe in Him. I don't ever want to think that the miracles in my life were done only for me. I recognize that I too have been equipped to perform miracles through your Holy Spirit. Every situation that needs a miracle will be done according to your will. Lord, you do miracles so great and for that I will Praise You.

My Prayer Requests for Today

Day 6
God's Love
(John 3:16)

The love of God is everlasting and transcends throughout eternity. His transforming love heals the broken hearted, gives sight to the blind and enables the lame to walk. It is the same love that Jesus shared with the multitudes. As a believer in Christ, fulfill your mandate to share this same transforming unconditional love with the people that you encounter daily.

Day 6 – Prayer

Father God you have given me nothing that I deserve. Why are you so merciful? You have loved me despite the fact that my sins are as scarlet. And only through the love of your son have my sins been washed white as snow. Your incomprehensible love is constant. Why have you loved me with an everlasting love? I can't understand your love? It is nothing like the love I experienced from the world. I thank you for your perfect love. I release you to show me how to love people the way you have called us to love one another. I do love you. Father with all my heart, my soul and my mind. Not only did you love me first, but you gave your only begotten Son, because you loved me. Hallelujah oh Lord.

My Prayer Requests for Today

_____

_____

_____

_____

_____

_____

_____

_____

_____

Day 7
Exceeding and Great Joy
(Psalms 43:4)

God has promised His children joy. The oil of joy is yours for the taking. Life's challenges don't have to weigh you down. God is the joy of your salvation, His joy will complete you. He will fill your heart with joy. He is our exceeding and great joy. Rise up child of God to experience the joy of the Lord as your strength.

Day 7 – Prayer

God of all I love to praise you. It is to you that I give the Glory, Honor and the Praise. I lift your name up high in all the earth. My Father, my King, my Lord you are my exceeding and great joy. All praise belongs to you. You have restored my joy and put a new song in my heart. From a far off I longed for you and here in your presence I experience the fullness of your joy. You promised me in your word that your gladness and joy will overtake even my enemies. Thank you Lord. I invite your presence knowing that the joy of the Lord is my strength. I need your joy in my midnight hour of praise, in the morning as I feel your breath of life within me, in the midday as you comfort me and even when I lay down my head as you give me rest. Your joy is welling up in side of me and cannot be contained. Lord I want to tell everyone about the joy that you have given me. Please release your joy to all of your children. With you there is no greater joy. You are the joy down in my soul. Hallelujah. Amen.

My Prayer Requests for Today

_____

_____

_____

_____

_____

_____

_____

_____

_____

Day 8
Rest
(Exodus 33:14)

God, the maker of heaven and earth knew that man would need rest. It is through resting that the believer is restored as a result of giving their reasonable service. God knew that man would need rest, that could only be found in Him. The privilege of resting in God allows the believer to be strengthened and empowered supernaturally. Rest in God today and be restored, by the only True and Living God. He beckons you to rest in His loving arms.

Day 8 – Prayer

Precious Father, I thank you for allowing me to have rest in you. This day has seemed endless. But now I can come boldly before your throne to speak of your grace and mercy towards me and to enter into your place of perfect rest. At this very hour I need your supernatural rest. I am content as you allow me to rest from the world and rest from serving in your Kingdom. I know that when I rest in your presence, you grant me the privilege of receiving a fresh outpouring of your spirit as you rejuvenate, revive and restore my mind, body and spirit. I am grateful for you pouring back into your servant all that I have poured out into your Kingdom, which is my reasonable service. When I rest in you I know that all that I need will be done to bring me back to the place of miraculous health, fit and ready for the master's use. Thank you Lord that I may lean upon the Mighty Breasted one, and feel your loving arms embrace me. Amen.

My Prayer Requests for Today

_____

_____

_____

_____

_____

_____

_____

_____

_____

Day 9
If He said it will He not do it
(Numbers 23:19)

L ife is always changing. It is good to know that the word of God remains the same. His word has existed for thousands of years. God never goes back on His word because He and His word are one. He is the same yesterday, today and forever more. Trust Him to be consistently faithful to you. God is a Faithful God. He watches over His word to perform it.

Day 9 – Prayer

Father God you have always been faithful unto me. Thank you for showing me that every word you have spoken to me is true. Even the Bible that you inspired the Apostles to write has proven to be true, time and time again. Because of your love for me you left your word as part of my inheritance. I am forever grateful for each word that has been spoken. These words have been spoken directly to me about circumstances I would encounter. Your word is filled with blessings, direction, power life, peace, joy, protection, knowledge, wisdom, safety and supernatural strength to defeat the adversary. You have even spoken some words to me personally that are for a time that is yet to come. I know that your word shall not return unto you void. You watch over your word to perform it. I trust you at your word and I depend upon a fresh impartation of your word daily. Thank you Lord for every promise you have spoken to me through your word. Glory to the Lamb.

My Prayer Requests for Today

_____

_____

_____

_____

_____

_____

_____

_____

_____

Day 10
The Exchange
(Isaiah 63:11)

Have you ever wanted to take back something to the store after you had purchased it? That's what happens when you accept things that don't belong to you, like a bad attitude or corrupt thoughts. God allows us to make a spiritual exchange of items that He did not create for us to have. In exchange for the negative things He allows us to receive replacements for bad purchases that we have brought.

Day 10 - Prayer

Oh Lord my God, how excellent is your name in all the earth. I see your mighty acts and I cry out Holy, Holy, Holy is the Lord God Almighty. I extol your name in the sanctuary and acknowledge your omnipotent power. You have shown me your power to conduct a spiritual exchange, which goes beyond my natural comprehension. How is it that you are able to give me beauty for ashes, the oil of joy for mourning and the garment of praise for the spirit of heaviness? You are all powerful. I cannot measure your faithfulness towards me. I now know that the negative situations that I have encountered cannot hold me down because they have had an encounter with you. What the enemy meant for evil, you are transforming it for my good. You have set me free from the chains that have bound me. I will only be subject to the Spirit of Christ, which dwells richly in me. Thank you Lord for exchanging my unnecessary baggage and exchanging it for freedom through your spirit.

My Prayer Requests for Today

_____

_____

_____

_____

_____

_____

_____

_____

_____

Day 11
Preparation for Fulfillment
(Lamentations 2:17)

In preparation to the fulfillment of your calling, every Christian will go through a process. These uncomfortable processes require you to accomplish the extraordinary "only" through God's help. He has designed the steps and season for the process to be completed in you. As a believer it is necessary for you to work in God's Kingdom. Submit to the process to fulfill your purpose.

Day 11 - Prayer

Dear Father, I have witnessed your magnificence today and you have shown me your Glory. How excellent is your name in all the earth. You told me in your word that you have the plans for me, so in you I put my trust. How beautiful it is that the creator of all creation has created me, with a divine purpose in mind. I trust that you are preparing me to fulfill my purpose. The steps that you have designed for my preparation have strengthened me along the journey, for the many obstacles that are before me. It is by your grace that I have come through the refiner's fire. The things in me that cannot be used in your Kingdom were taken from me during my process. I trust that I am now ready to perform the work you have required me to do, because you God have prepared me for Kingdom fulfillment. Even my heart has been prepared for a more intimate relationship with you for the fulfillment of my purpose. Hallelujah to the King. Amen.

My Prayer Requests for Today

Day 12
God's Word Concerning You
(Psalm 138:8)

Daily seek the word of the Lord for direction, power and strength. As we pray and come before God's throne He unveils the answers to our petitions, in His word. Never doubt that He will answer. He is concerned about the things that concern you.

Day 12 – Prayer

Lord God, everything you do in my life is perfect. You are my pure delight. I sing praises to your Holy name, for your name is great and greatly to be praised. Thank you for loving me and being concerned about me. Just knowing that you are concerned about the things that concern me put my spirit at rest. From the smallest to the largest aspects of my life, you are interested about them. You have Lordship over every area of my life. How gracious you are to me. You have told me that you watch over every hair on my head. Thank you Lord. You've declared your faithfulness over where I walk, by ordering my steps. Thank you Lord. You have commanded specific things concerning me because I am your child. For this I am convinced that you see all, know all, can do all and are concerned about all the things that concern me. Thank you for your Lordship concerning me. To God be the Glory for the things you have done.

My Prayer Requests for Today

_____

_____

_____

_____

_____

_____

_____

_____

Day 13
Get the Vision
(Proverbs 29:18)

God has a specific vision designed for all of His people. As you mature spiritually He will share this vision with you. He doesn't allow us to lose track of the vision. He helps you to retain the vision in a variety of ways. Remain focused and aspire towards fulfilling your destiny. Grab hold of God's vision for your life and accept the greater work that He has called you to do.

Day 13 - Prayer

Lord Jesus, at your name every knee shall bow and every tongue shall confess that you are Lord. Thank you for the vision you have declared for my life. Through this vision you have called me to do great and mighty things I have yet to comprehend. I acknowledge that your vision for my life is far greater than my own. Lord, your vision for me is exceedingly and abundantly above all that I can ask or think. When you spoke forth the vision for my life you opened doors that no man can shut and you shut doors that no man can open. Your vision for my life has direction. I know that the vision is for an appointed time, but in the end it shall speak and not tarry. Thank you for manifesting every detail necessary to fulfill the vision for my life. You are making the path for the vision clearer every day. Thank you Lord. Therefore, be it unto me to seek after your vision for my life and not my vision. I know that there is life in your vision. Glory to Your Name.

My Prayer Requests for Today

_____

_____

_____

_____

_____

_____

_____

_____

_____

Day 14
Strength for the Weary
(2 Corinthians 12:9)

Every believer needs God's supernatural strength. This strength is not limited to spiritual, physical or mental. It is for so many areas of your life. There may be times in your Christian walk when you need God's strength to hold you up because you feel yourself falling, to encourage you through difficult times and to sustain you even in the dry places. Be comforted by knowing that God will give strength to the weary.

Day 14 – Prayer

All praise belongs to our God. For He alone is worthy to be adored. From the mountaintop you have declared in your word that you give strength to the weary. Thank you for showing me that I can overcome all weariness by looking towards you Lord Jesus. By waiting patiently on you, remembering your promises, declaring your word and being consistent in my faith walk, you are strengthening me each day. Oh Lord, I thank you. I will not be weary in well doing for in due season I will reap and faint not. You are strengthening my thoughts, physical body and my abilities to share the Gospel of Jesus Christ to your people. I am full of your spirit and He is leading me. Thank you Lord. Today Oh Lord I can run and not get weary. You have given me the Victory and supernatural stamina to push through adversity and stand in the most difficult of situations. Again I thank you Lord. This day is full of your Glory.

My Prayer Requests for Today

Day 15
A Pastor's Heart
(Jeremiah 3:15)

A Pastor is one who has been divinely appointed and anointed to watch over God's people. They are given the responsibility to lead God's sheep and love them unconditionally - while laying down their lives for them. Pray daily for God to sustain the Heart and Purpose of your Pastor so that they are continually encouraged to minister God's word to His people.

Day 15 - Prayer

Father, your love is perfect and beautiful. I celebrate your Holiness. You have anointed a Pastor to be a faithful shepherd over my life and the life of my family. Father your servant Pastors are men and women after your heart, who lead me with knowledge and understanding. Father please encourage, provide, protect, maintain, vindicate and unconditionally love them. Impart wisdom unto them. Enlarge their territory. Help them to be more like you, destroy strongholds that come against their lives, forgive them, grant them grace and mercy, guide their footsteps, fight their battles, root and ground them in love. Make them strong like a tree planted by the rivers of water that bringeth forth fruit in its season. Reignite their fire for ministry and soul winning. Use them as oracles to set the captives free. Give them a passion for prayer. Help them to be more sensitive to your spirit. Most of all cover their heart for it holds the unconditional love for your people. In Jesus Name!

My Prayer Requests for Today

_____

_____

_____

_____

_____

_____

_____

_____

_____

Day 16
God's Order
(Psalm 119:133)

God has predestined every believer. He has strategically and sovereignly placed you at specific places during particular time because of the order He has established for His Kingdom. God had specific purposes in mind to Glorify Him, when He ordered all of His creation to come forth. His order is perfect. Obediently walk in the destiny that He has ordered for you.

Day 16 – Prayer

Praise be unto God who has made heaven and earth. In you Heavenly Father I have everything that I need. From the beginning of time you established order for your Kingdom. You arranged the order of the stars in the sky, the animals on the land, the fish in the sea and the dominion of your children on the earth. Order has been commanded by you in the place where my family and I share your love and testify of your grace and mercy. This order extends into your temple where I worship and celebrate your Holiness. Together with your sons and daughters - we call forth order in your Kingdom and pull down every imagination and every high thing that exalts itself against the knowledge of Christ. You have also declared order inside of me- within this temple where your spirit resides. I submit to the order you require me to follow, which is my reasonable service. Because of the priestly order of Melchizedek I have salvation through your son Jesus Christ. Amen.

My Prayer Requests for Today

_____

_____

_____

_____

_____

_____

_____

_____

_____

Day 17
I Can Do All Things
(Philippians 4:13)

J uggling the demands of the day can sometimes be difficult. To complete the work that God has given to you for this day, there are resources provided and spiritual discipline necessary. At times physical endurance is needed. These tasks can be completed when we faithfully rely upon God's grace and God's word. He has promised that it can be done through us, and that "We can do all things through Christ that strengths us."

Day 17 – Prayer

Gracious God, I sing praises to your name. Sovereignly you have directed me to complete so many assignments in your name. Lord, I have found that completing Kingdom assignments have not always been easy. I thank you Lord, because through prayer all of your work gets done. You have equipped me with your anointing and given me the tools needed, through the gifts of your Holy Spirit to complete every task. Daily you prioritize every task and they are accomplished. Oh I Thank you. Lord, please keep me steadfast unmovable always abiding in your works. Father as your instrument for service, I submit myself to you for the building of your Kingdom. Your word has declared unto me that I can do all things through Christ that strengthens me. There is nothing too hard for my God and who dwells richly in me. Therefore, the things that seem impossible with man are possible with you. I praise you for your divine abilities.

My Prayer Requests for Today

_____

_____

_____

_____

_____

_____

_____

_____

_____

Day 18
Draw Unto God
(James 4:8)

When you have an overwhelming desire to come before God it is a spiritual manifestation from the Holy Spirit of God. He is letting you know that He is drawing you to spend time with Him, so that you may hear clearly from God. The more sensitive you are to His spirit, the more you will hear God beckoning you to come into His presence. Draw closer to God and He will draw closer to you.

Day 18 – Prayer

King of Kings and Lord of Lords I sing praises to your name. For your name is great and greatly to be praised. I welcome a fresh infilling of your Holy Spirit daily. Each day I anticipate a glorious day with you as your spirit leads, guides and directs me. I can't do the work that you have created me to do without your spirit. Father, I thank you for the purpose of your spirit to reveal all truths and teach all things. Having the privilege of your spirit that rests, rules and abides within me is an honor. Daily you are making me attuned to your spirit. I often feel your Spirit calling me to come before your presence. I appreciate you calling me to partake of your Holiness. In your presence there is fullness of joy and at your right hand there are pleasures forever more. I look forward to the time spent with you where I may dwell before you, bask in your presence and sing your praises. When you call upon me I will answer thee and draw close unto thee. Amen.

My Prayer Requests for Today

_____

_____

_____

_____

_____

_____

_____

_____

_____

Day 19
His Strength is Made Perfect
(2 Corinthians 12:9)

God knows the exact amount of His strength you need to make it through each situation. He knows where His strength is needed most in your life, how to apply it and when to apply it. This reflects the sovereign nature of God. He'll utilize His omnipotent strength, which is made perfect in your weakness. His strength is far greater than your abilities.

Day 19 – Prayer

O h Lord my God you are all praiseworthy. I am awestruck of this brand new day. Lord I can't thank you enough for your strength. I am encouraged knowing that throughout my life your strength is all I need. Your strength sustains me. When I am weak you are strong. Your word declares unto me that the joy of the Lord is my strength. In the midst of my battles you are my strength and my shield. Time and time again you have shown me that you are my refuge and my strength. Because of your strength I need not be afraid of ever being strong enough, because your strength is made perfect in my weakness. Therefore I rejoice in you. Blessed be Your Name.

My Prayer Requests for Today

_____

_____

_____

_____

_____

_____

_____

_____

_____

Day 20
Peace in the Storm
(Mark 4:39)

Storms of life blow daily and come in different ways. Your life as a believer will never be absent from storms. Each storm affects us differently. Jesus said that we could speak "Peace Be Still" to every storm. God has given you the power and the authority to speak to your storms. Use God's power and take dominion over the wind and the waves. Your storms are subject to the words you speak. Command peace for your storms.

Day 20 - Prayer

God you are great and greatly to be praised. From the rising of the sun you are worthy of my praise. This day through your power, I declare your word over my life. You told me to speak to the mountain - be thou removed and you told me to speak to my storm - "peace be still" and it shall be. By your word you have given me the power to speak those things that are not as though they were. I have the power of life and death in my tongue. Therefore I command and decree "life" according to your word. For this I praise you. I speak abundant life over me, my family, those in leadership over me and your entire Kingdom. This day I decree that doors shall open that no man can shut and that doors shall shut that no man can open. You have given me the authority to take back every territory that the adversary has taken from me and that he must return a double portion back to me. I speak that I am subject only to the Spirit of Christ. To the Spirit of strife, distraction, confusion, and chaos, I speak *"peace be still."* In Jesus' Name!

My Prayer Requests for Today

_____

_____

_____

_____

_____

_____

_____

_____

_____

Day 21
God's Faithfulness
(Psalm 40:10)

God cannot fail. He is faithful to you and the covenant He made to all His people. Victories in the life of the believer come as a result of God's faithfulness and are manifested by our faith in Jesus Christ. God has called and created you. Believe that God is faithful and will remain faithful unto you throughout eternity.

Day 21- Prayer

Praise be unto our God. He alone is worthy of all our Praises. Father I am forever grateful for your faithfulness unto me. You are noble, you are honorable and you are true. You are not a man that you would lie. Every word you have spoken shall come to pass. Neither are you the son of man that you would repent. You are perfect and Holy in all of your ways. Thank you for giving me your son as an example to lead me in righteousness. Gracious God you watch over every one of your words to perform them. You govern over each word making sure that each word comes to pass. Your word does not return unto you void. Therefore each word is carried out according to your divine plan. I have found promises in your word declaring unto me that you would never leave me nor forsake me. Father, this shows your exemplary faithfulness over every aspect of my life. Daily I can trust and depend upon you more. You are faithful. Hallelujah.

My Prayer Requests for Today

_____

_____

_____

_____

_____

_____

_____

_____

Day 22
Restoration
(Psalm 23:3)

God's ways are not our ways. He sees the plight of His children and meets every one of your needs, including restoration. His restorative power will replenishes and transforms your heart, mind and physical body. God restores by re-establishing what He has already placed within us. Invite God to replenish you. He can even restore your soul.

Day 22 - Prayer

Praise God from whom all blessings flow. New mercies I see every morning. Lord where I am weak you are strong. It is to you I give the glory. I need your restoration today, right now, at this moment. Renew me in the depths of the places that I have covered over with a mask. For too long I have tried to hide my infirmities, weaknesses, inabilities and shortcomings. You knew these things all along and you were waiting for me to acknowledge and confess them to you. Thank you Lord. I yield to your restorative power that refreshes the empty places needing your strength, infilling of your spirit and power. Daily I depend upon you to be my breath of life, daily bread and living water. My day is not complete without you. I need your continuous restoration daily. Thank you Lord for bringing me back to life by the death of your Son. I praise you for your restoration and I sing Glory to your name. Thank you Lord for being there for me.

My Prayer Requests for Today

_____

_____

_____

_____

_____

_____

_____

_____

_____

Day 23
Set the Precedent
(John 13:15)

The sons and daughters of God are placed strategically within the earth to make a difference for the cause of Jesus Christ. Wherever you are positioned, your purpose is to Glorify God. The world watches everywhere you go, everything you do and everything you say. In whatever setting God has placed you in today, take the opportunity to share God's word and set a precedent for His Kingdom. God's will shall be done in Heaven and in the Earth.

Day 23- Prayer

Blessings and Honor belong to the King. Hallelujah. God, the master plan for your Kingdom is that you be Glorified, the Gospel be spread by your people, that I obediently follow the commands you have established and that we - your children prosper and be in good health even as our soul prospers. In the beginning you set plans into motion with rules to govern your Kingdom. Thank you for enabling me to obediently observe your commands. I am under the new covenant and not under the law. However I must account to you for the things that I think, say and do, because I am subject to your command. Within your precepts I find grace and mercy. Please help me to set the precedent to bring forth your Glory. In every destination that you have directed me I will fulfill my purpose whether I am in the workplace, home, church, and community. Lord, I Thank you for considering me for this task and allowing me to walk in the paths you have commanded to set the precedent. All Glory is due to your name.

My Prayer Requests for Today

_____

_____

_____

_____

_____

_____

_____

_____

_____

Day 24
No More Struggle
(Psalms 3:8)

Israel struggled for 40 years as they wandered in the wilderness. There was conflict among the tribes and blatant disobedience. Because of this, many of God's chosen people never made it to the promised land. God has designed some situations so that when you come into the place of your promise, you will appreciate His leading you out of the struggle and into your purpose.

Day 24 - Prayer

Father, How great thou art. How great thou art. As a Christian I have had more struggles than I care to count. Often I have seen that the major struggles that I experienced are within me. So I ask in the name of Jesus that you would keep me from evil. Some of the struggles have seemed insurmountable. But you Oh God have shown me that you are victorious over every one of my struggles, when I put my hope and trust in you. Therefore, I submit every struggle to you right now knowing that I have the victory in Jesus' Holy Name. You mighty God have shown me that I wrestle not against flesh and blood but against principalities, against powers, against rulers of darkness, spiritual wickedness in high places throughout my struggles. Lord, I know that some of my struggles have been designed by you to make me more God-dependent, instead of me being self-reliant. I now see the purpose of struggling. Thank you Lord. Now as I journey, even in my own struggles, I know that you lead me through the journey and lead me out undefeated. Amen.

My Prayer Requests for Today

_____

_____

_____

_____

_____

_____

_____

_____

_____

Day 25
Victory
(1 Corinthians 15:57)

God has called every Christian to possess a victorious life. In this life you will have struggles including wars and battles. Everyday there are challenges in your life. They are all subject to the Spirit of Christ that dwells within us. There is nothing that you endure for Christ's sake, that God has not already given you the Victory over. Today walk in victory and declare in the atmosphere words of victory over every area of your life and receive your victory through Christ.

Day 25 - Prayer

Oh Lord, I magnify your name in all the earth. You are highly exalted. Father you are omnipotent, omniscient and omnipresent. With every breath I proclaim that you are all powerful, all knowing, everywhere and in every step that I take in your name. Thank you for the steps of victory by which Christ has set me free. Every day I am confident of my victory over the snares and traps that the evil one has set before me. You would not have me to be unaware of satan's devices. Therefore you have given me discernment and warn me of stumbling blocks placed before me. I will always have the victory in Jesus Name. My victory was won on Calvary's cross and paid for by the blood of Jesus the Christ. I declare victory over every demonic stronghold that has come against my life. No weapon formed against me shall prosper. Father I seek your supernatural instruments in my battles for victory. I will use the sword of the Spirit which is the word of God. Strong holds and yolks formed against me are destroyed. Hallelujah, for the victory. Amen.

My Prayer Requests for Today

Day 26
Laying at His Feet
(Luke 10:38)

The Bible tells us the story of Mary and Martha. One sister desired to be a servant and the other chose to lay at the feet of Jesus. As a believer in Christ you too must establish priorities for serving in the Kingdom of God. Lying at Jesus' feet must be a priority over working in God's Kingdom. Cultivate your relationship with Jesus and spend more time in His presence, which is most important.

Day 26 – Prayer

lory to the Lamb. The precious Lamb of God. Your compassion fails not. Thank you Lord for my purpose as a believer, which is to work in your vineyard to build your Kingdom. Too often I have chosen to be busy doing work in the vineyard instead of lying at the feet of your son and my Lord Jesus Christ. As I lay down at the feet of Jesus He is perfecting me. Thank you Lord. In Your presence You reveal to me my purpose, develop the power within me through your Holy Spirit, grants victory through Christ Jesus, provide direction, peace, joy, love and fulfillment for my life. For this I thank you Lord. Please help me to make it a priority of diligently seeking you. By doing this I know that I can be effective ministering your words of "life." Father I know that you give all of your children free will. For me there is no other option that I desire, over spending time in your presence, worshipping, praising praying and reading your word. Thank you Lord for allowing me to have access to the feet of Jesus. Glory.

My Prayer Requests for Today

_____

_____

_____

_____

_____

_____

_____

_____

Day 27
Guard Your Heart
(Proverbs 4: 23)

God created the heart of man and woman to be sensitive towards happiness, love, joy, hurts, pains, disappointments and to other emotions that we encounter throughout our day. He admonishes believers to protect their heart by using Godly wisdom and follow His direction. It's because of His mercies that we are not consumed by our feelings. Therefore, don't risk pouring out words of destruction from your heart into the Kingdom of God. Beloved guard your heart.

Day 27 – Prayer

Heavenly Father, great is your mercy towards me. Great is your grace. Thank you for knowing what would take place in my life before the beginning of time. I have had so many challenging situations where my emotions have become casualties of war. This day I give you every situation and I decree your word that states, "I shall not die but live to declare the works of the Lord." The situations that have hurt and encamped my heart cannot destroy me. God you love me with an everlasting love and your love makes me complete. I recognize that these words are from your heart for my heart. There are no more strongholds that affect my heart. If there is anything that remains within my heart it must be subject to the spirit of Christ that dwells within me. Purify the life that flows out of my heart and make it clean and Holy. My heart is not contaminated. The words that you have given to me to speak to your people are full of life. In Jesus' Holy Name. Amen.

My Prayer Requests for Today

_____

_____

_____

_____

_____

_____

_____

_____

_____

Day 28
Behold the Works of His Hands
(Psalms 46:8)

How beautiful are the works of the Lord. Singing birds, the tapestry of blue skies, the diversity of His people. Even the intricate features of hillsides illuminate these works. He has created each one, for His good pleasure. Praise God for His mighty works. Thank God for the marvelous work He has created in *you*.

Day 28 – Prayer

Oh Lord my God you are a wonder to behold. This is the day that you have made and I will rejoice and be glad in it. I will declare your wonders throughout all generations. Your outstretched hands have unveiled your majesty in the Heavens and within the earth. I see before me the beauty of your Holiness. Thank you for allowing me to witness your omnipotence. Surely, all of these wonders that have come before me, have come from you. You are the one who is perfect in knowledge. I will tell everyone how you have granted me the privilege to witness all of your splendor. Your wonderful deeds far outweigh my abilities. I will daily mediate on your works. You have spoke and all of creation has come forth to show your divine sovereignty. Your creation is a wonder to behold. Thank you Lord, for even I am fearfully and wonderfully made. Marvelous are thy works. No one can perfect your perfection. Your works illuminate the atmosphere for all of creation to behold your Glory.

My Prayer Requests for Today

Day 29
Thy Will Be Done
(Luke 11:2-4)

The Lord's Prayer specifically states "God's will be done." When the children of God disobey God's will, don't think for a moment that His will won't get done. It will get done because He says that it will. The task that He has predestined you to do to will get done, if not by you, it will be done by someone else. Know that God will choose an obedient believer to faithfully carry out His will, His way, to Glorify Him.

Day 29 – Prayer

Blessings and Glory belong to our God. Father, I believe that prayer is the core of our relationship. You have given me prayer as a means of communication, from you to me and from me to you. Thank you Father for leaving instructions on how to pray in your Holy word. Within that same word you have shown me your divine ability to complete what you have established for your Kingdom. As I meditate on your word I believe that, "thy Kingdom come, thy will be done." Thank you Lord for giving me the responsibility to complete the work that will edify your Kingdom and give you the Glory. Thank you for considering me a faithful servant that will follow through and complete the assignment that you have predestined me to accomplish. I don't want anyone else to do for you what you have entrusted me to do. I count it a privilege that you would choose me. Lord, I ask for your help to do my part, for thy will to be done through me.

My Prayer Requests for Today

_____

_____

_____

_____

_____

_____

_____

_____

Day 30
Looking for Love,
He loved us First
(John 3:16)

We often look for love from others to fill a void that only God can fill. It is only God who can quench our indescribable thirst and the longing in our hearts. The Love that God has for you, His child, can never be duplicated by human efforts. His love for you is so great that He sacrificed His only son to die for you. He did this because He first loved us.

Day 30 – Prayer

L ift the Savior up. For years I have looked towards man/woman to love me and to fulfill my heart's desire. Too many times I found myself longing for fulfillment of a need that was unquenchable by human means. Your revelation knowledge has helped me to understand that the emptiness, yearning for fulfillment and desire for love could only be quenched through you and not man. You have allowed me to partake of your love, which is perfect and beautiful. Thank you for giving me eternal life from the beginning of time through the sacrificial love of your son. Father you told me that I must "love the Lord my God with all of my heart, my soul and my mind." I do love you. Your word also declared that love is patient, kind, does not envy or boast, is not proud or rude or self seeking, is not easily angered, keeps no record of wrongs, does not delight in evil but rejoices with the truth, protects, always trusts, hopes and perseveres. Lord your love is perfect. Thank you for your decrees of love.

My Prayer Requests for Today

_____

_____

_____

_____

_____

_____

_____

_____

Day 31
A Season to Bear Fruit
(Ecclesiastics 3:1)

Within the Life of every believer God will take you through many seasons. There are seasons to sow and seasons to bear fruit. Whichever season you are in right now, it is part of the plan of God. Stand strong while you are sowing seeds into God's Kingdom and watch your seed bare fruit, in its season.

Day 31 – Prayer

Gracious Redeemer, Glorious Lord. Your word declares unto me that "there is a time for everything, and a season for every activity under heaven." I praise you Lord because I know you have ordered every step I take. My journeys have designated beginnings and designated endings. You have promised me that you will send rain in due season. Hallelujah. I will praise you all of my days. My latter rain will be greater. Even my wilderness experiences have an expected end with a specific season. I shall be like a tree planted by the rivers of water that bringeth forth it's fruit in my season. Thank you Lord for the season that has prepared me to bring forth fruit. It was during this season that you broke up my fallow ground and enabled me to speak your word in confidence of the calling that you have placed upon my life. In this season you manifested your word that declares that, "in due season I will reap if I faint not. Thank you Lord for allowing me to glorify you. Amen.

My Prayer Requests for Today

_____

_____

_____

_____

_____

_____

_____

_____

_____

_____

Day 32
Decently and in Order
(1 Corinthians 14:40)

Whenever there is more than one person making a decision there will always be differing of opinions. God's rules however command that all things, be conducted decently and in order. By following the Lord we honor the one who sits on the throne, who reigns in majesty. God is not a God of confusion nor discord. Follow the rules and standards that He has established for His Kingdom here on earth.

Day 32 – Prayer

God of all, creator of all creation, I worship you. Everything in your Kingdom you called forth in order, according to your perfect design. Order sets the precedent for the work of your creation. When you spoke your word into existence you established order for every branch of your church. You expect everything to be conducted in excellence, because our Kingdom work represents your Kingdom. I declare that order surround me always and not confusion. Gracious God your word has declared that "You" have ordered my steps in your word. So, with that divine revelation I acknowledge that every word that I need will come at the right time with a divine revelation. Therefore, when I read your word I will fully comprehend it's truths revealed by your Holy Spirit. Thank you Lord. Nothing in my life happened as a result of happenstance. I trust that you have structured every aspect of my life within a path where your precepts will be conducted decently and in order.

My Prayer Requests for Today

_____

_____

_____

_____

_____

_____

_____

_____

_____

Day 33
Do the Work of the Lord
(John 6:28-29)

God created man to do assignments within the earth. He has equipped us with all of the necessary tools and resources to complete the task. The gifts He has placed within you helps to build His Kingdom. When God calls you with an assignment, answer Him. The equipment is there, He's just looking for the one who'll say *"yes, I'll be a willing vessel for you God."* Amen.

Day 33 – Prayer

Lord God, you deserve all the Glory and Honor. Thank you for every morning. Father you called me to worship and praise you and to do the work that you have specifically equipped me to do. There have been times when you have called upon me and I have hesitated or not moved in the direction that you have predestined me to edify your Kingdom. Please forgive me Father. I repent. In my heart I know that the work you have specified for me to do, no one else was created to do. Have mercy upon me Lord. I realize the importance of spreading the Gospel of Jesus Christ and edifying your Kingdom. Thank you for calling my name to help you. You are so powerful and mighty that you could have done it without me. But you chose me Lord. Thank you Lord for considering this servant. I say yes to doing the work you've called me to do. I shall do it through the help of your spirit without hesitation. In Jesus' Name. I will listen for and take direction from your Holy Spirit. Amen.

My Prayer Requests for Today

Day 34
The Chastening of the Lord
(Revelations 3:19)

Every Christian is born into sin. God in all of His mercy allowed us to be forgiven our sin through confession and repentance. God's love for His children does not keep us from receiving chastening for our rebellious acts. In God we will never receive the full punishment deserved, but we will receive His chastening love. Today, thank God for His merciful chastening.

Day 34- Prayer

Heavenly Father, thank you for loving me. Your love is unconditional. You loved me before I could love myself and you loved me despite what I did and who I was. The things that I have done are in my past and are now covered under the blood. Thank you for your forgiveness. Father I know that even in your forgiveness of my sin you will chastise me. You chastise me because you love me Lord. Help me to walk a Holy life circumspectly always in obedience to your word. If I should fall short of your Glory I would prefer to receive your chastening because it will be more merciful than the chastisement of the world. While I walk in this Christian journey I pray that you would show me when I am wrong so that I may submit my offenses upon the altar to you. Then you can once and for all destroy the yolks that have attached themselves to me. It is my earnest desire to walk with your help in wisdom, knowledge and understanding through your Spirit. Amen.

My Prayer Requests for Today

Day 35
The Transcendental Life
(Job 11:7)

As a child of the Most High God you have the privilege to live a transcendental life. Walking obediently with the Lord, God is able to perform the incomprehensible, do the incredible, create the impossible, and reveal the unfathomable. He is able to do all of these things and so much more because He is God. The possibilities with God are endless. On this day, *experience* the Lord of Lords who has no limits.

Day 35 – Prayer

Glory to the King. You are the one that is, that was and is yet to come. The more I draw closer to you, the more I desire to spend more time with you in prayer. You have taught me that in prayer you require me to be still and listen for you to reveal things beyond my understanding. By meditating on your word you reveal supernatural revelation and knowledge with me. Please give me the spiritual discipline to accomplish this. Intimate moments spent with you have revealed great and unsearchable things I did not know. Thank you Father for this privilege and honor. Prayer and meditation enables my life to go beyond the ordinary limits as my thoughts are being transformed. Your word living within me takes over my intellect. There are some things that don't line up in the natural, but I am walking by faith and not by sight. I am unlearning some things in the natural and comprehending other things in the spirit. Thank you Lord for this revelation given by your Spirit.

'

My Prayer Requests for Today

_____

_____

_____

_____

_____

_____

_____

_____

_____

Day 36
Strengthen thy brethren
(Luke 22:32)

God specializes in the restoration of the hearts, minds, bodies and souls of His people. His infinite abilities bring His children back to their place of health and spiritual stability. Trust that God will never leave you in a dysfunctional state. He will even anoint other believers to help restore and strengthen His Kingdom, within you.

Day 36 – Prayer

Father you're abiding faithfulness leaves me in awe. Thank you for your restorative powers. There have been times in my life where I have felt like an eggshell shattered into a million pieces. You have been merciful, picked up all of my pieces regardless of their shapes, healed my wounds and restored me. You Lord are the great physician penetrating the deep places within me to grant me mental, physical and spiritual restoration through your love. Thank you for your mercy Lord. By Jesus' stripes I am healed and no longer broken. Today, this day, I receive supernatural healing from your Son. By faith, deliverance and victory are mine through Christ Jesus. And now with my hope in Him I will be used as your vessel to take this same spirit of healing and apply it to the wounds of my brothers for them to be healed and restored. Amen.

My Prayer Requests for Today

_____

_____

_____

_____

_____

_____

_____

_____

_____

Day 37
God's Favor
(Genesis 18:3)

God in all of His majesty desires to bless His children with favor. God grants favor as He pleases. It cannot be earned by anyone or any means. As a believer in Christ know that the favor of God rests upon you. God commands so many situations to come together for your good. This is the favor of God. His favor is a privilege for every believer.

Day 37 – Prayer

Beautiful Lord, I thank you for your Favor. All the days of my life I pray that I may find favor in your sight. There is nothing that I can do to receive your favor. It is your sovereign ability as Lord over my life to grant me favor. I am so very grateful to receive your many gifts, generous acts of kindness, assistance and preferential treatment. This very same favor was granted to your people during their wilderness journey. Praise be unto your name. Jesus, you alone have allowed me to have a connection to the one that can change the hearts and minds of man. Right before my eyes you speak your word and manifest your favor. Your power transforms man to grant me favor on your behalf. Lord I thank you for the ability to be connected with you and to partake of this divine relationship. In this relationship with you I know that I can depend upon you. How awesome you are. It is good to know that I can count on you Father to manifest your favor in my life. Amen.

My Prayer Requests for Today

Day 38
He will command His Angels
(Psalms 91:11)

The children of God have angels specifically assigned to them for healing, as warriors in battle, to be messengers and for other assignments. God Himself has commanded His angels to guard and watch over you. Therefore, in your uprising and in your going down you are never alone. Call upon the angels that God has commanded to watch over you.

Day 38 – Prayer

Precious Lord, All Glory belongs to you. For strength to walk during this Christian journey you have given me your Son, your Holy Spirit and you have even commanded angels to watch over me. Thank you Father. Because you are the creator of all creation your omniscience goes even into the heavenly realm. You created innumerable heavenly beings, your angels who are known for their great abilities. Specifically your angels Michael, Gabriel, and Raphael defend, protect, provide, guide and act as ministering servants in my life. Thank you Lord for every one of your angels that you have commanded over my life. You dispatch them to encamp me and defeat the enemy on my behalf. I am thankful that I may call upon them daily to request their assistance in any situation that I am faced with. Thank you Lord for these ministering spirits that fight in the Heavenlies to free me from the destructive works of satan. Hallelujah to our King.

My Prayer Requests for Today

_____

_____

_____

_____

_____

_____

_____

_____

_____

Day 39
Unexpected Blessings
(Leviticus 25:21)

Anticipate a move of God that will send an unexpected blessing to you at anytime and from anywhere. As a child of God you should start each day being open to receive His unexpected blessings. When you least expect a blessing, God will open up His storehouse and bless you in ways you can't imagine. Anticipate that He will do it. Get ready for His unexpected blessings.

Day 39 – Prayer

Lord, thou art worthy to be praised. Your Holy word declares your Magnificence and your Glory. You have been with me every step of this journey. You know what I want and what I need. At this very moment I am experiencing a mighty move of your power. You have taken my breath away. My prayers along this journey have been for freedom, spiritual breakthroughs, and deliverance, for your people, your Holy Nation, your Kingdom. I have even asked for a closer relationship with you because I desire a deeper intimacy with you. You have given me blessings that I have not expected and in no way anticipated or deserved. I am overwhelmed at the fact that you would consider giving me an unexpected blessing. You knew what I desired without me even asking you. I could not do anything to deserve your beautiful unexpected blessings. You have given them to me only out of your love for me. Thank you for your innumerable unforeseen grace. All Glory belongs to your name.

My Prayer Requests for Today

_____

_____

_____

_____

_____

_____

_____

_____

_____

Day 40
Abundant Grace
(2 Corinthians 4:15)

Coming into the place of Abundant Grace, God quickly multiplies the blessings you know you don't deserve. Blessings overtake you and overflow in such a manner that you cannot contain them. Recognize that these blessings have come not through your own means, but by God's Grace. It is here that you Praise God abundantly and receive His Abundant Grace.

Day 40 - Prayer

Lord of all, I sing of your love and your abundant grace. Glory to the King. Lord you have been with me in the mountains high and the valleys low. Thank you Lord. Right before my eyes you are unveiling a new horizon. I hear the sound of the abundance of rain. It is overtaking me and running me over. I feel the saturation of your rain and I praise your Holy Name. Rain is falling from the Heavenlies bringing to pass every word that you have spoken. Father you have given me grace to grow through this journey and your grace has kept me while you perfected and cultivated me for your Glory. Your loving kindness and grace has been far greater than I deserve. Through prayer, praise and worship you have allowed me to walk into the place of Abundant Grace. I bow before the King who has lead me through still waters, covered me under your wings and allowed me to dwell in your secret place. Thank you for the privilege to receive your Abundant Grace. Glory to the King.

My Prayer Requests for Today

Conclusion

Prayer and fasting are biblical principals that should be readily functioning in the New Testament church. God called His nations into agreement to witness the manifestation of His power. Individual and corporate prayers are answered as a result of fasting. I urge every believer to fast at the leading of the Holy Spirit and seek the face of God. In that place Jesus will transform lives and circumstances. God promised that "If my people who are called by my name, would humble themselves and pray and seek my face and turn from their wicked ways, then will I hear from heaven and will forgive their sin and will heal their land," 2 Chronicles 7:14. God will do the impossible.

By partaking of this fast and journaling daily, a record of the manifestation of God in the lives of a nation was documented. God's word instructed me to, "*Go now, write it on a tablet for them, inscribe it on a scroll, that for the days to come it may be an everlasting witness," Isaiah 30: 8.* I pray that God is glorified by the fruit of this labor.

About the Author

Elder Kim Y. Jackson is a native of Baltimore, Maryland. She is an anointed writer, conference speaker, teacher, oracle and psalmist for the Lord. Through the power of the Holy Spirit Elder Jackson imparts revelation knowledge to empower believers in Christ. As an oracle and scribe for the Lord, God has released her to effectively minister in the areas of healing and deliverance. Elder Jackson ministers at several recovery houses, transitional homes and support groups.

She is called to write the plans of God for His people. Her self-published books include *In the Garden*, *True Worship - Understanding the Command of God for a Chosen People* and *Forty Days of Grace.* She has also contributed to the anthologies *This Far by Faith*, *Have a Little Faith* and *Keeping the Faith*. Elder Jackson is also the founder of the Women Writers of God's Word Authors Tour.

Elder Jackson has fully accepted her calling to preach, write for the Lord, teach God's word and spread the Gospel of Jesus Christ. She stands on God's word and encourages other believers to "Write the Vision" (Habakkuk 2:2) and follow the vision that God has given to them.

Elder Kim Y. Jackson has a Masters Degree in Divinity, Bachelors Degree in Christian Education and an Associate's degree in Biblical Studies from the Family Bible Ministries Worldwide, Institute, College, Seminary, School of Counseling and University. She also has a Bachelor of Arts degree from the University of Maryland, Baltimore County.

For more information about booking for speaking engagements or for ordering books please email: writethevizn@aol.com or go to www.writethevizn.webs.com._

Write the Vision and Make it Plain
Habakkuk 2:2-3

Made in the USA
Middletown, DE
04 April 2023

27678563R00080